1983

Lydia B. Hodgson

Made with ❤ on the BookLeaf Publishing Platform
www.bookleafpub.in
www.bookleafpub.com

Dedication

For Morgan, Jacob, & Sydney.
You have brought more love into my life than I ever thought possible. I am so proud of the compassionate, kind, beautiful souls you are & I love you always.

Preface

Words don't magically appear on a page. Sometimes, they flow easily; every thought works. Other times, they kick, claw, and twist on their way out. This book has been the latter.

These poems generally span a particular period of my life. I didn't necessarily intend that, but that's the beautiful thing about writing. Sometimes, the words lead us along despite our best-laid plans. Much like my first work, each poem in this book is a piece of my story - a reflection of where I was, how I felt, and what I experienced.

Once again, I hope you will connect with this work, find echoes of yourself in its words, or maybe gain a new perspective on your journey.

Thank you for taking the time to read my work. I hope these poems bring you as much solace and joy in reading as they have brought me in writing them.

Acknowledgements

To Joey: Thank you for being the loudest cheerleader in the room, always. Seeing myself through your eyes, even brief glimpses, is fuel to keep going. I love you.

To my kids: You are the reason I do everything. If you work for it, absolutely anything you want is possible. Don't let the world make you smaller.

To my girls: You are everything. I love you doesn't even cover it. Thank you for your wisdom, friendship, advice, strength, long text messages, longer phone calls, etc. Just thank you.

To my parents: Thank you for loving me. It was enough.

1. Dollhouse

In a quiet corner of the yellow sunlit room,
Where shadows play and flowers bloom,
Stands a dollhouse, crafted with care,
A gift of love, beyond compare.

With hands that once soothed lullabies,
A grandmother built it, under starlit skies.
Her tools were simple, her heart was true,
Each piece a memory, old and new.

The tiny windows, framed with gold,
Hold stories yet to be told.
A rocking chair, a table, a bed,
Dreams alive where dolls are led.

She papered the walls with gentle hues,
Soft pastels, pinks, and blues.
Tiny curtains stitched with lace,
A cozy hearth, a warm embrace.

The girl would sit, her eyes alight,
Exploring worlds both day and night.
In that house, her stories grew,
Of queens and knights, of skies so blue.

The grandmother watched with a knowing smile,
Each doll placed with tender style.
For in the house, she saw her own,
A childhood past, seeds she'd sown.

The dollhouse stands, a bridge in time,
A bond eternal, pure, sublime.
A legacy carved in wood and thread,
Where love resides and dreams are fed.

2. Bunny Cake

A little realm of warmth and light,
Where mornings yield to soft delight—
The fragrant air, a sugared spell,
Enchants the space we knew so well.

The Bunny Cake, a sacred rite,
With whiskers spun from licorice night—
Its frosting clouds, a snowy gleam,
Adorning Easter's cherished dream.

We shelled the peas, we shucked the corn,
Our fingers green from husks well-worn;
Her hands, like time, both swift and slow,
Taught mine the art of kneading dough.

The biscuits rise, a golden crest,
By my grandmothers's hand, they were always best;
Each crumb a memory, sweet and mild,
Of love that binds both kin and child.

Sacred hearth, where time stands still,
Where laughter lingers, hearts refill—
In my grandmother's kitchen, life's refrain
Was baked in love, and sung again.

3. Boxes

The frost was harsh, the air was keen,
The world a stark and brittle scene—
When we returned, the silence spoke,
In tones of parting, hearts half-broke.

The walls that held our laughter's hue,
Now bore the gray of fleeting view;
Each box a coffin for the past,
Each corner echoed—leaving, fast.

The hearth, once warm, no longer glowed,
Its ashes cold, its fire stowed;
Our footsteps trailed through brittle snow,
To bid a hurried, faint adieu.

The friends we'd held in tender trust,
Fell to the wind, as all things must;
A wave, a tear, a fleeting cry—
The bonds of youth to winter fly.

The house, now strange, grew small, grew dim,
A specter of what once had been;
And yet, within its shadowed frame,
The ghosts of home still breathed our names.

Through icy panes, the world withdrew,
Its edges sharp, its colors few—
And as we left, the silence burned,
A winter's truth—we won't return.

4. Pal-cakes

We left the lanes of sugarcane fields,
The kindly trees that knew us well;
The morning stretched, an endless thread,
Through miles that held a tale to tell.

The bridge rose high, a silver arc,
Above a river deep and wide;
Its waters spoke of dreams untold,
And worlds that waited, open-eyed.

The Pal-cakes sign, a broken blue grin,
Hung bright upon the distant air;
It whispered of adventures near,
And sweets that only courage dares.

The house loomed cold—a giant's keep,
Its empty hall a quiet shroud;
Yet echoes whispered, faint and soft,
Of joy to come, both bright and loud.

The lawns stood clipped, like velvet seas,
Each blade aligned with stern regard;
The streets were strange, yet humming low,
With life that seemed both close and far.

Oh, child's heart, so quick to fear,
Yet quicker still to seek the new;
The city's pulse, a grand refrain,
Calls tender souls to rise and bloom.

5. Stranger

They led me to a foreign place—
Its walls were tall, its windows bright;
The voices rose, a practiced tune,
I faltered in their lofty flight.

The desks aligned in perfect rows,
Each one a castle of its own;
Their rulers knew what I did not,
Their whispers carved in sterner stone.

The words they spoke were strange to me,
Each one a riddle, sharp and cold;
Their books were maps of distant worlds,
Too vast for seven years to hold.

The city roared beyond the glass,
Its current pulled, a restless sea;
While I, adrift, could only watch—
The waves too quick, too far for me.

No daisies graced this concrete yard,
No bayous to hum, no fences to climb;
Just shadowed towers, stoic, mute,
And bells that marked the march of time.

Yet somewhere in the quiet air,
A tiny spark begins to glow;
Perhaps, within these strange new halls,
A seed of knowing starts to grow.

For even strangers, lonely, small,
May find their voice, their steady hand;
And weave their roots in foreign soil,
To flourish in a distant land.

6. Kitchen Song

I left the fields of cane and corn,
The rooster's call at crack of morn,
The barnyard smells, the tractor's drone,
And now I feel so far from home.

The city hums, a buzzing hive,
But I don't feel alive, alive.
The roads are gray, the skies are cold—
The stories here are strange and old.

But when the world feels big and mean,
I find the place where I've been seen.
The kitchen whispers, soft and sweet,
Of my grandmother's voice and kneading wheat.

I sift the flour, the sugar flows,
The butter soft, the cinnamon glows.
The bowl becomes my hiding place,
A flour-dusted, warm embrace.

The oven hums, a kindly tune,
Like crickets in the heat of June.
Each cookie, pie, and loaf of bread,
Is like a hug from words she said.

And though I'm far from fields I knew,
From morning skies of silver blue,
The smell of bread will always be
The farm that lives inside of me.

7. Sanctuary

I found a haven, still and small,
Within the shadowed, silent hall;
The words a balm, the page a key,
To realms of calm unknown to me.

When tempests rose within my door,
And thunder rolled from roof to floor,
I sought the shelves, a sacred space,
And vanished from the fray's embrace.

The ink became a guiding hand,
To take me through a kinder land;
Where forests whispered, oceans gleamed,
And life was woven as I dreamed.

No chaos could invade this place,
No heavy hand, no scornful face;
The books stood steadfast, brave and true,
A world apart, yet vast and new.

Each spine a sanctuary bright,
Each chapter built with tender light;
And though my soul was worn and thin,
They wrapped me gently, safe within.

So let the world be harsh and loud,
Its voices sharp, its burdens proud;
The solace of the page remains,
A refuge from life's stinging pains.

8. Ink

The page is quiet, but it listens well,
a confessional of bleached white silence.
I spill my thoughts like a slow-falling tide,
black ink washing over hidden wounds.

Each word, a weight once buried deep,
unearthed with trembling, steady hands.
Sentences stretch like aching limbs,
reaching for light beyond the storm.

The pen absolves what the tongue withholds,
bleeding sorrow in careful lines.
Punctuation halts my restless ghosts,
full stops like prayers for restless minds.

By the final stroke, the air feels clean,
the echoes softer, the past unchained.
The paper bears what I no longer must—
a quiet mercy, a weight released.

9. Creosote

The old bridge still lingers in memory's haze,
its creosote scent thick as the summer heat,
sharp and tar-black, rising in waves
as the boards groaned beneath bare feet.

I was small then, rod in hand,
toes tracing splinters in rough-hewn planks,
where dragonflies hovered in golden bands
and the bayou shimmered, slow and dank.

Poppie's voice, patient and low as the tide,
warned of water moccasins coiled below,
but I only listened to the bobber's glide,
the hush of current, the warm wind's flow.

Sun-beat afternoons bled into dusk,
mosquito hum soft as a lullaby.
I swore the bridge would never rust,
never fade, never say goodbye.

But time has a way of wearing wood thin,
like footprints washed from the earth's embrace.
Still, when the air turns thick again,
I catch the scent—and see the place.

10. Unwritten

She moves like a shadow through silent rooms,
small hands tracing the edge of the past.
The walls hum with voices that do not call her name,
bottles whisper where laughter should last.

Her father sleeps when the world is awake,
his love a tired ghost, warm but dim.
She presses her ear to the hush of his breath,
wishing the hours would bend for him.

At school, she drifts in a sea of new faces,
their laughter a language she cannot speak.
The city is loud, but she fades in its clamor,
a ghost of the girl she used to be.

So she hides in the margins, ink-stained and safe,
folding herself between pages and lines.
If no one will listen, the paper will hold her—
a world where her voice is defined.

And maybe one day, they'll open her books,
see the girl they once let slip through.
Read her voice in letters of longing,
and know she was there, waiting too.

11. Melody

In a room where shadows softly creep,
A young girl sits, too tired to weep,
Her world a blur of distant sound,
Where echoes fall but hearts aren't found.

Yet in the silence, faint and clear,
A fragile note slips past her fear,
A thread of gold, a whispered plea,
The melody—her company.

Each chord, a bridge across the void,
Each beat, a pulse she once destroyed,
But now it hums within her chest,
A borrowed heart, a place to rest.

The music wraps around her thin,
A woven cloak stitched deep within,
Its rise, her breath; its fall, her sigh,
A language soft enough to cry.

She dances where no feet have been,
In rooms carved out from notes and skin,
The chaos fades, the noise grows small—
In melody, she's found it all.

12. The Sweater

She wears it like a second skin,
Threadbare arms to fold her in,
Stretched too wide, sleeves past her hands—
A quiet house, a silent stand.

Faded threads, a stitched disguise,
A place to tuck her shrinking size,
Loose enough to blur the lines,
Hide the heart she can't define.

Father's gone before the light,
Chasing days, outpacing night.
Mother drifts in bottled seas,
Eyes like windows, lost of keys.

So she pulls the sweater tighter still,
A fabric shield, a fragile will,
Hoping she might just dissolve,
A ghost with nothing left to solve.

No one asks, and she won't say
How soft things slowly slip away.
But in the seams, her quiet plea:
If you don't look, you won't see me.

13. Visit

Down the gravel road, the silence grows,
Fields lean dry where the cold wind blows.
She grips the air, thin as thread,
On her way to where grief has spread.

The farmhouse sags beneath the sky,
Windows dim, curtains shy.
Inside, the walls remember more
Than voices do, or hearts restore.

Her grandmother lies in a fragile frame,
A brittle shell, a whispered name.
Hands like paper, soft and worn,
Folding time, mending torn.

Her bare head rests on cotton thin,
Skin stretched tight, bones caving in.
Tired eyes, glassy, distant, wide—
Searching for something she left inside.

The girl sits close but speaks no word,
Fearing how small her voice sounds, unheard.
So she holds those fragile hands instead,
Touching all the things unsaid.

Outside, the wind forgets to care,
But in that room, grief fills the air—
Not loud, not sharp, just faint and slow,
Like roots beneath the frost and snow.

14. Heavy

The room is thick with wilted air,
Heavy with flowers that do not care,
And something sharper, raw, defiled—
The bitter sting of formaldehyde.

She stands, fists clenched, beside the glass,
Staring through to a hollowed past.
Her grandmother lies too still, too neat,
Waxy skin, cold hands, shrunken feet.

This isn't her—the woman who grew
Roses tall and skies so blue,
Whose laugh was stitched in summer's seams,
Whose voice still echoes in her dreams.

Now darkness blooms where light once stayed,
A heavy thing that will not fade.
It's in her chest, behind her eyes,
A shadow that no tear can disguise.

She's angry at the silence kept,
At words unsaid, at nights she wept
While her mother folded into grief,
A distant shape, sharp-edged, and brief.

There's no space for both their pain—
No bridge to cross, no words to name.
So she swallows rage like jagged stone,
Carrying it, heavy, alone.

The coffin closes with a sigh,
A soft goodbye that feels like a lie.
Darkness follows where she roams,
Because she's lost the place called *home*.

15. The Sink

The kitchen isn't yours, she thinks,
Hands clenched tight around the sink,
Fingers stained with citrus, peel—
Proof of every scraped-together meal.

Where were you when the pots boiled dry,
When dinners burned and nights slipped by?
When cereal or frozen pot pie counted as a feast,
And silence grew, piece by piece?

Now they hover, sleeves rolled neat,
Claiming counters, shuffling feet,
Measuring flour like it's some grace,
Like absence isn't hard to trace.

They quit drinking, found their way—
But I lived here every day.
This oven knows my bitter heat,
The floorboards echo with my defeat.

I carved myself from bread and bone,
Taught the stove to feel like home.
Now they stir like none of it stayed,
Like healing's just a debt repaid.

But the scars don't soften when you knead,
And hunger's not just lack of need.
So don't call this a fresh new start—
The kitchen knows. So does my heart.

16. Echoes

The porch sags where we once sat,
shelling peas into metal bowls,
feet swinging over sun-warmed wood,
the hush of dusk settling in slow.

Wind hums through the broken screen,
whispers of laughter caught in its fray.
Dust dances in the amber light,
stirred by ghosts of yesterday.

The floorboards creak in greeting,
their voices softer than I recall.
Faded curtains breathe with the wind,
as if the house still dreams at all.

The kitchen smells of memories—
biscuits rising, coffee strong.
A clock that never told the time
ticks in silence, ticking wrong.

Out past the fence, the fields remain,
golden, endless, stretching wide.
The echoes of my younger self
run barefoot through the countryside.

And though the years have pulled me far,
I feel them here, I feel them still—
the voices, hands, the love, the past,
held forever in these walls.

17. Magic

Barefoot on sun-cracked roads,
we march to the rhythm of cicadas,
heat waves dancing ahead,
asphalt sticky, tar bubbles begging—
pop, snap, laughter echoing.

Fences become our ladders,
hands gripping weathered wood,
grass stains marking knees
like badges earned, proof of courage.

We climb trees that touch the sky,
leaves whispering ancient secrets,
feet dangling, hearts pounding,
masters of a leafy universe.

Beneath a willow's sweeping veil,
we carve kingdoms from shadows,
weaving tales in tangled roots,
mud pies and dandelion crowns—
our fortress hidden from time.

Fields stretch beyond our knowing,
oceans of green and golden sway,

and we, brave explorers, trace paths
through wildflowers and whispering corn.

The world is endless in our eyes,
every rustle a mystery,
every breeze a promise—
that summer never fades,
and neither will we.

18. Mountains

We rumble up winding roads,
past trees so tall they touch the sky.
Dad says we're almost there,
and I press my face to the window,
waiting for the mountains to let us in.

The air smells like pine and river,
cool and sharp in my nose.
The trout stream hums over smooth gray rocks,
water so cold it bites my toes,
moss slick under my stumbling steps.

Fog drifts low in the early morning,
a ghost that comes and goes,
curling over the water,
then slipping away like a secret.

At night, the fire crackles and snaps,
flames licking blackened pots,
marshmallows bubbling, faces glowing,
stories dancing in the dark.

We sleep in a tent that smells like rain,
wrapped in blankets, listening—

to owls calling, crickets singing,
the hush of the mountains
holding us close.

19. Corked

She learns young—
how to shape her lips just right,
curve them upward, make them light,
a smile smooth as glass.

Laughter floats above the table,
thin and weightless,
while voices crack like thunder
just down the hall.

She corks herself tight,
shoves every want, every need
into a bottle deep inside—
no room for spillages here.

If she stays quiet,
if she stays good,
maybe the storm won't notice her,
maybe the walls will hold.

But sometimes, late at night,
when no one's watching,
she presses her fingers to her ribs,
feeling the swell beneath—

pressure rising, glass straining.

She wonders how long
a bottle can hold
before the cork gives way,
before everything spills.

So she smiles a little brighter,
laughs a little louder,
and twists the cork in tighter.

20. Elsewhere

She dreams of elsewhere—
somewhere beyond the dust-thick air,
beyond the worn-out voices
that forget to say her name.

At night, she maps escape routes
in the folds of her blankets,
imagines roads unspooling like ribbons,
leading to a life where she matters.

She is a ghost in her own home,
floating through rooms unseen,
words caught in her throat like birds
too tangled to fly free.

She knows they love her—
in the way the sun loves the earth,
distant, steady, unaware
of the shadows it forgets to touch.

She does not have the words
to ask for more, to be more,
so she builds another life in her mind,
where doors open when she enters,

where someone is waiting on the other side.

And until then, she keeps dreaming,
keeps pretending, keeps planning—
waiting for the day
when elsewhere
becomes real.

21. Enough

I used to think love was something soft,
something easy, something sure.
But now I know—
love can be tired hands and quiet apologies,
love can be broken things, still trying to hold.

I grew up in the cracks of their sorrow,
learning to tiptoe through silence,
to read the weight in their voices,
to swallow my own.

But time has a way of opening doors,
letting light into places once shadowed.
And now, with years behind me,
with children of my own—
I see them clearer than before.

They loved me in the ways they knew,
in the dinners at the table,
in the worn-out lullabies,
in staying when leaving might've been easier.

I did better, yes,
softened the edges,

held my children close,
listened more, shouted less—
but I wasn't perfect either.

Now, when I see them,
we do not speak of the past in apologies.
We sit, we laugh, we love—
in the way we always did,
in the way we always knew how.

And that is enough.

www.ingramcontent.com/pod-product-compliance
Lightning Source LLC
LaVergne TN
LVHW021314200726
843509LV00012B/1919